In Search *of*

Dustie-Fute

DAVID KINLOCH

CARCANET

First published in Great Britain in 2017 by

Carcanet Press Ltd

Alliance House, 30 Cross Street

Manchester M2 7AQ

www.carcanet.co.uk

A CIP catalogue record for this book is available
from the British Library: ISBN 9781784103965.

Typeset by Richard Skelton.
Printed and bound in England by SRP Ltd.

The publisher acknowledges financial assistance
from Arts Council England.

Supported using public funding by
**ARTS COUNCIL
ENGLAND**

IN SEARCH *of* DUSTIE-FUTE

Also by DAVID KINLOCH
from Carcanet Press

Finger of a Frenchman · 2011
In My Father's House · 2005
Un Tour d'Ecosse · 2001

Contents

In Search of Dustie-Fute

I, Giraffe

Sous le pont Mirabeau coule la Seine

APOLLINAIRE

I, Giraffe, *camelopardalis*,
once dappled, high on mimosa trees,
raft and dam this second flood:

they hammer feverishly beside me,
– Lilliputians with their guys and ropes –
tautening an ark against the ever-rising Seine;
a dilute version of Gustave Eiffel's tower
emerges like Leviathan:
a scaffolding to save or break

my neck. Yesterday I lost sensation
in my feet but fret not, for this heart
has pressure valves large enough
to lock down oceans of my blood.
Stand proud, my father said, *we may be lifers
in a zoo but they have made a guddle
of this damp city and all the world beyond.*

Once, he told me how we all began:
Giraffa of the order Artiodactyla
were trees that moved and got their spots
from strolling through the leaves
that left their shade on them.

He spoke of a creature called 'savannah',
rich in acacia and a delicious
whistling thorn; the resident oxpecker
which roamed his person like a daemon

for unwanted ticks, the black piapicks
that sieved the air for insects.

It has begun to stink. This morning
I spied a rat swim past my right hind leg.
Small fires dot the cityscape
and a man shuffles on two chairs
across the deluge. He says: *This is a street.*

There is no river here. And drowns.
A minute iceberg crowns his debris.

Now even the gas lighters have gone
and it is dark as the bush at sunset.
Paris is a city of pontoons and floating *passerelles*
and I nap uneasily as small punts prowl
the outskirts of our zoo. At ten, I woke
to see them float the hippopotamus away,
his rump bulbous in the moonlight.
Yet he could have swum!

Ghosts of my hunted ancestors haunt my dreams:
Baringos impressed for buttons, Rothschilds
reduced to thread and guitar strings,
the bladder of a Hock stitched for a water bag.
Parisians! I am a simple reticulated camel-cow
and abjure aristocratic forbears.
I am not good to eat! Waterlogged and knobbly
I shiver as dawn floods the abandoned garden.

★

It is too late. My squire the donkey
makes final obeisance in a sympathetic
neigh: *Passe avant, sieur Sarapha!*
Move on now to the next world.

This earth is all unstitched
its colours washed away.

So I swing my head along the arc
of all my longing.
The rivers' waters move like wings about me,
the days thrash; my single leg
– icy, seraphically numb –
harrows this flood like a pestle.

I pass; I pass; the days remain,
rain-washed, hand in hand.
Rivers become the towers,
hooves of all the little people
bob among the eddies;
upended trees, dishevelled wigs
root among the waves.

Doused hopefulness
of this long, slow life;
love comes and goes
and goes; the days remain.

The Parawd o Dustie-Fute

DUSTIE-FUTE
eftir Eugenio de Andrade

He cam fae a fremmit land,
had kent thrist an the watter o Mairch bere,
his feet i the wey o the slaw stour o eternitie.

The dour snaw cam eftir.

GREATER HORSESHOE BAT

Rhinolophus feurrumequinum!
Soon you'll be extinct as Latin.
Your horseshoe noseleaf
Sculpts the ultrasound of Gaia's grief.

AYE-AYE

To us the Aye-Aye is a no-no,
A lemur like a tiny academic:
Big starey eyes, bat ears, baldly hirsute, it knows
The jury's out; scary, peaky, rainforest geek.

LEAR'S MACAW

Lear sketched your blues:
Wished you a Boss-Woss, a Pobble or Jumbly;
You parrot his limericks humbly:
There was a   there was a   there was a
Caged mostly in pea-green zoos.

                                    MAN

                          Shaped like a pumpkin
                          Lardy and farty and screwy
                          and a pure mingin killer
                          Makes the ocean floor a bin
              Hypocrite lecteur, mon semblable, mon frère.

DUSTIE-FUTE

Tae apen hauns.
As if the wun war the mairvel.
Tae straik the outloup o his mane,
lently the lent fever craig.

Tae let him lae,
still green.
Wi the outpour,
cream o the well.

                                    THE DHOLE

                          The Dhole's a wild dug
                          That clucks lik a hen:
                          He's loast his fuckin habitat
                          An the habit o rhyme.

THE BLUE WHALE

Big on omega 3, I gulp
9,000 pounds of plankton per day;
Pavarotti of the sea, I belt
it out: bray spray, spray prey,
outweigh everyone!

DUSTIE-FUTE

Whan she glowered
back intae thi pit

than ma shouders gowped,
ilka stab lik thi clash o an aik

ilka faa lik the glisk
o lichtnin fused

i the mirk.

Noo the nicht-hawk
flauchters thru brainches,

deeback an leesions
hap ma hide,

the parawd
intae the untholeable licht.

THE SNOW LEOPARD

What can the leopard tell us of snow?
That it is melting away.
What does the snow say of the leopard?
It has melted away.

DUSTIE-FUTE

Now Dustie-Fute is Nemo
Trees and beasts ex-beau
Hot bod hard-got
But a liar the light forgot.

Orpheus

After a treated photograph by F. Holland Day

1.

All ways the underworld
is all stone never song
no matter how you search in it.

Nor are we out of it;
say it; you cannot sing
it. The rocky head that dreams

from an outcrop across
the Aegean is stone.
The boy flexing his muscles

against a gash in the hill
digs the road — a butterfly
wavers, grass stirs —

the ash that soars like a flute
beside him is a pylon.
You look back

at your lifelong companion:
stone
ash

2.

Deep in the galleries
he looked back
unguided

never at the portraits
– almost never –
but at the hieroglyphs
that aped them
in panels
tiny echoes

he could make no sense of.

3.

In the evening
when the wood joists
holding it all up
gleamed like wheat
and off-lighting

he could see her – or him – exactly.

Yes, it was him
– or her –
that is his nose
her jaw – precisely.

It is clearly how it was
in that world

in this

4.

piped music   endless prose

5.

It wasn't hell
but an endless art gallery
full of pictures of his friends
or acquaintances
– yes, acquaintances –
just as they were in life.

6.

He noticed
how little the limbs seemed to matter
in portraits
mere furniture propping the head

While before
outside
they had been almost
everything

7.

He took notes:
two or three
words
per line

trying
to make
songs
again

8.

The Russian composer of *Pictures at an Exhibition* sat on a bench before *A Hut on Hens' Legs* by Victor Hartmann. He looked hard. It took him the whole tour to realise that he, Modest Mussorgsky, was Eurydice, his cherubic, bloated face staring back from all the pictures, that he was the thread through all the images, making them glow like wheat, fluttering like a butterfly among them.

Arrow-Men

After a magazine illustration by J. C. Leyendecker

All I can see of Joe's face lost
behind the paper is its newsprint,
billowing out like sail
or lyre, so thirled to his
sedentary form his head
is simply headlines, leader
articles, ads for the *Arrow*
shirts and collars we illustrate.
Illustrations, that's all we are,
and if there's 'lustre' or
'illustrious' embedded here,
there's also 'lust' and 'ill'.

Well, we're Big Sixes,
Joe College and Joe Yale,
cat's pyjamas, whiskers, meow,
the butterfly's boots
to the baby vamps
and bug-eyed Bettys
who write to us in thousands
every week. I mean we're
just sketches, Doll, all
dolled up in shantung silk,
sacque suits for summer,
choice bits of calico in our way.
You can have us in crash motor
coats, dust-proof and durable.
Our bosoms pack these backless
waistcoats with a swell
that well sets off the Earl
and Wilson semi-stiff.

We never crease;
our bit of flannel's imperturbable.

None of my beeswax, but
do I know you? You stare and stare
and before you turn
away to go to bed, glance nervously
at the book face-down
between my full-back hands.
Then you kiss our gloss.
We never seem to notice though;
Joe never makes
his point about the market.
But if you didn't go to bed
what then? Would it be
a fashionable tale or a tale
after our fashion? Would it
go like this: boy loses girl,
searches for her to the ends
of Earth, turns round
at the last minute, loses
her again and here we are
in this upholstered limbo,
shades of our former selves?
Maybe? I almost believe
the story. Joe does, don't you
Joe? Though we can't quite
get it right; like it's in a language
we never fully understood and so
we turn from one translation
to another, like clothes
at a fashion shoot,
mugging up in case they
ever question us.

Once, we compared versions.
My lines go like this:
'And when suddenly
the god stopped her and, with anguish in his cry,
spoke the words: *He has turned round* –
she understood nothing and said softly: *Who?*'
Never mind the god's identity.
I try, I am trying to remember
if that pause after the deft colon
was really there, and was it
hers or mine? Once, Joe, you took
the book gently from me
and it came out a little differently:
'So that, when suddenly the God stopped short,
took both her hands in his and said
with pity in his voice: *He has looked back!*
She did not follow him, murmured: *Who?*'
In this one there are her hands,
his hands, pity, murmur, nothing
soft. Now there are just Joe's hands
and mine. Let's pull ourselves
together, eh Joe, my Joe, old Joe?
We're butch and beautiful.
Forget the girls?
They'll strip us limb from limb.

Joseph's Dreams

1

Call

Not mine. The call wasn't for me. The phone
rang in the next room and it was the Angel.
Can I speak to Mary? I heard the voice
in my head, soft as the chisel edge
that scalped my thumb in carpentry at school;
I got anti-tetanus and penicillin in each
buttock and fainted. I've never heard
Mary as quiet. The silence
is like blown glass. My wife and the Angel
glowing, long-life bulbs electrified
by prayer. So I imagine. I spend
a lot of time imagining: children
or at least a child.

2

Annunciation

The angel wrote the word
with his finger right
on her eardrum,
tickling the wax.

I spoke to her
picturing the vowels
and consonants
in the pale unlit canals.

She beseeched me
with her eyes
and we folded our hands
in silence.

3

The boy

I teach him. He is grateful.
Holds love back for a future
as big as this nail
I beat into the bench
where it lies almost
flush with the wood.

4

The Language of Flowers

At the school's annual General Knowledge Quiz
they asked *Which flowers burst forth from Joseph's rod?*
I wrote *Ask the dove*
but was marked wrong.

Now I know the answer.
It was acacia blossom
mixed with marigold and cactus,
topped by bittersweet.

The internet url is
thelanguageofflowers.com

no spaces.

5

Puppet

I've cut myself a puppet.
He looks just like Jesus.
Rosy cheeks, long hair
and he speaks in parables.

Whenever Mary comes
he cries *Screw you bitch!*

Whenever Jesus
Fuck you, baby!

Oh Baby.
When is a puppet wood?
When is it flesh?

6

Joseph's Demons

Demons are nesting in the electricity box.
A sure sign. I prize the sticky mess
free of the wood and kill the speckled eggs.

I can hear the electrics
– the angels' frequency –
their uplifting chatter.

Go into Egypt
Big Telephony commands.

7

A Dream

In my dream, my son does not take me
by the hand but I take his.

The crumbs on the kitchen table
can be picked at and eaten,
not swept away in case
of visitors continually expected.

And in my dream, up there
is where my proper life goes on
and I embrace the insubstantial
family who ache for my ascension
to that cloud rife with greenery,
mango trees, mixed weather
and a love devoid of words.

8

Lifeline

It's not the DTS.
A miniature earthquake
splits my lifeline.

The donkey's ears
grip tight to the sky.

She turns my hand
over and over
like a pancake.

When I hold her face
it slaws off,
jiggered and unending
into the scrub.

9

St Joseph's Dream

In all the pictures I am sleeping:
dozing on a rock, snoring by a candle.
She, of course, got to shake
hands with the Angel.

I woke with the kind of boner
I haven't had in decades
and expected a larger life,
less falling asleep on the job.

I've dreamt each big decision:
the move down south to Egypt,
the sidey-ways turn to Galilee.

The boy dreams too. Just
to look at him, though,
I can see I don't feature in his.

What use are dreams really
if you're the one asleep in them?

10

Another Dream

Sometimes I dream my dreams are simple
palimpsests of sun through cloud.
But in my dream I may not dream
of dreams, and the sun is a perpetual light
switched on so I can act
in this strange, gilded world
where rulers work as terrorists
and hunt my perfect son.

Flee into Egypt, voices say.
Or *Rest here. Dream here.*
Where the water is pellucid
as the voice that speaks my dream.

I wake but the dream continues.
I look into Egypt's dust
and see the plain deal table
in the kitchen back at home,
a woman who's half familiar,
and a simple boy
looking up at me with adoration.

11

Rainbow

The coat of many colours belonged
to another Joseph
and he didn't predict your tweeds,
your avuncular worsteds.

Put on the cape,
shake out the gamp,
tell your students
how to spell galoshes.

You'll wait for the train with your son.
You'll try to tell him you have
cancer and you love him.
He cannot bear your emotion.

12

Noli me tangere

The painter has given my son
an extra finger. My mistake.

13

Branches

I had no flowers to give
her, no diadem, no throne,
just branches the colour of
the wood I used to hew
and one from that crew
detached itself and grew
miraculously
to mock me
into a thorny crown.

Lichtung

After The Clearing *by Andrew Wyeth*

Everything is falling, pouring onto the switch-
grass and the Sweet Joe Pye Weed.

Shoulders cascade upon his torso and the tan line
pulls tight the stack of thighs.

Ferns bunch about his genitals, his cock a cut
above the avocado of his balls; his pubic hair

writhes up in streaks of luminescence. He glows
against the dark break of the conifers.

Behind, the sea is there and tiny zephyrs
still whirr about his long blond hair.

Arnold's stats compel the sheepish
copy of plain words and simple statements.

Here is Venus, rising from the back
pasture, his strong girl's face

insisting you receive him as he is.
Yes. He has a history: just yesterday

he slept with both boys by the riverside;
his Warhol screen test went up

in smoke and mirrors; he leapt
five stories down and was broken in.

The phosphorescence of his limbs
is the glitter of putrescence:

sand dollars, shiners dying as he rose.
His shell is wholly clear now

for this encounter.

The bachelor stripped bare by his brides, even

After a portrait of Marcel Duchamp by Florine Stettheimer

If I place my eye to the peep-
hole in this rock, I can just
make out his head staring
back at me from the borders
of the morning. Light
suspends it, blinds me
as I again unpack the shadows.
Who would have gone with him?
In order to descend that never-
ending staircase and pass
through the smallest crevice
he planed his limbs so they could be
closer to me at every moment.
He shed beauty like a snake,
skinned his retina so no pleasure
could take root. Infra-
thin rouge on lips was all
that told me he was there.
That and his suitcase...
an album with his latest
songs perhaps, or space
for me... It was touching
if I could still be touched.
But I was an idea now
and when he turned to me,
wrapped in his coat,
it was just to share the thought
that two blue threads floating
from his sleeve could help
him measure chance.
What was he thinking?

I turned away, back
into the diagram of caverns.

Still, I see that head
in my mind's eye,
like a bicycle wheel
attached to a stool
spinning out the same
song, same thread,
same net. I raise
up my arms and slip
nothing on.

Installation

After 'Untitled': Portrait of Ross in L.A. by Felix Gonzales-Torres

And he took the big glass jar, smashed it and gave the sweeties to them, saying:

This is my pear drop, this is my pan drop, this is my soor ploom, this is my humbug, this is my fizzy belt, this is my wham bar, this is my caramac, this is my fizz stick, this is my sherbet dab, this is my pineapple chunk, this is my mint imperial, this is my jelly bean, this is my jelly baby, this is my gummy bear, this is my floral gum, this is my dolly mixture, this is my love heart, this is my aniseed ball, this is my rhubarb and custard, this is my kola cube, this is my black jack, this is my sweet tobacco, this is my chocolate coin, this is my foam mushroom, this is my milk gum, this is my space dust, this is my pint pot, this is my liquorice pip, this is my popping candy, this is my coconut log, this is my marshmallow, this is my foamy teeth, this is my giant tongue, this is my terror eye, this is my barley sugar, this is my butterscotch, this is my curly wurly, this is my fizzy grizzly, this is my giant rat, this is my scented satin, this is my mahoosive jumbo gobstopper, this is my funny face, this is my scary skeleton, this is my rainbow pencil and this my edible paper

given for you.

Do this in memory of Ross who once weighed 175 lb and only 37 lb at his death from AIDS in 1991.

Felix, June 5, 1994

After a photograph by A. A. Bronson

You thread a sea with your eye;
each time the needle enters your flank
the pain composes you;

trees that hung your voice
among these patterns
wrap your quilt in foliage;

a dog barks through the branches;
a girl's arm passes like an oar
across the sunlit patches;

now your song kneels
at the river's edge
and will not flow;

your passport head is pinned in silk.

For one last time then, the images of Orpheus or Dustie-Fute – as he was once called in these parts – coalesce. And some of these images are appropriate to A. A. Bronson's 'memento mori' for his late partner, the artist Feliz Partz, one of the largest photographs in the exhibition *Hide and Seek*. The dead man lies wide-eyed, staring out at us, mouth open as if in astonishment; but the quilts and rugs and pillows that surround and wrap him vie equally for our attention. They remind the viewer of the great AIDS quilt begun in 1985 which now comprises some fifty thousand woven panels, each one commemorating an individual who has died.

I say 'some of the images are appropriate' to make clear that this poem isn't new. It was first published in 1994, the very year Bronson made his photograph, and formed one of the final pieces in a long sequence called 'Dustie-Fute'. This mixed original elegies with adaptations, fragments of newspaper reports that first documented the outbreak of a strange new disease, as well as snippets from a medieval herbal. The aim was to create a text that was as patchwork as the commemorative quilt and suggest also the complex network of conditions that combined fatally to suppress the immune system of those they attacked. The sequence is now over twenty years old and the events it chronicles – the early years of the AIDS pandemic – over thirty. In a moment I'll explain why I reprint it rather than try to write a new poem in response to Bronson's image. It is also a fact that I cannot get beyond this image in my overall response to the series of portraits I have been writing about. I was going to write: 'these personal issues', but there is a sense in which they are not personal but general and akin in this respect to Bronson's own form of art practice summed up by the name he gave to his collaborative work with Partz and Jorge Zontal, *General Idea*.

But first, 'Felix' himself commands more attention. The visual image itself is quite large and takes up a good part of the wall of any gallery where it is hung. I haven't made an exact calculation but it is probably about the same size as the individual patches that make up the AIDS quilt which are three by six feet, roughly the size of a human grave. To this extent, therefore, it is the most extreme interpretation of the quilt's function. Assuming Bronson made the image partly with the AIDS quilt in mind – and this is far from certain – I wonder whether his aim was not slightly satiric: while it can be overwhelming to experience the quilt in person its mission can strike the viewer as softly commemorative, particularly when panels are viewed in isolation. Pathos is the emotion most readily induced.

But Bronson's art here is more visceral. He doesn't deal in metaphor and symbol as the makers of the quilt inevitably do. He more or less gives us the body of the deceased itself, pinning it to the wall of the gallery. What's more, the 'itself' is still, uncannily, a 'himself'. This is because the image is not complete without the explanatory description, provided by Bronson himself, which accompanies the photograph. The whole work is a mixture of image and text. There we discover that the photograph was taken in the hours immediately after Partz's death, that in the final stages of his various illnesses Partz suffered from extreme wasting of flesh and muscle and that it was impossible to close his eyes after he had died.

In the years since then, Bronson has given various interviews about his work and it has become clear that Partz was to some extent 'dressed' for this photograph and that it was a final act of collaborative art making by the two men. He has also spoken about Erwin Panofsky's work on tomb sculpture which he discovered after the photograph was taken and, although it could not have influenced the work itself, Bronson wishes to set it in the art historical context Panofsky evokes. In particular, Bronson mentions the late medieval phenomenon of the 'transi' or cadaver tombs in which an image of the deceased is presented as if in the process of decomposition.

Nevertheless, I believe that Panofsky's opening essay on Egyptian funerary art is at least as relevant and fits better with comments Bronson has made about the way Partz's life force seems to have drained off into the brilliantly coloured fabrics on the bed around him. Indeed, 'Felix' becomes an Egyptian in this photo. As Panofsky points out, the ancient Egyptians did the exact opposite from what seems natural after someone's death. They opened the eyes and the mouth so that the dead might see, speak, enjoy whatever type of afterlife was available to them. And they tried to make the dead happy by providing the necessities of food, drink, locomotion, service, all placed within the shelter of tombs that were often constructed as if they were houses.

So, if you look closely at the photograph you will see that 'Felix' lies just within reach of some of his favourite gadgets and personal items: his cigarettes, his tape-recorder, the remote control for the TV, all objects that will come in handy in the millennia ahead.

Bronson closes his explanatory description with the following invocation: *Dear Felix, by the act of exhibiting this image I declare that we are no longer of one mind, one body. I return you to General Idea's world of mass media, there to function without me.* 'General Idea' in this context perhaps bears some relation to Egyptian *Chū* or, as Panofsky expresses it, 'general world-soul'. So Bronson's photo is not so much commemorative as what Panofsky calls 'prospective' or 'projective'.

Like the ancient Egyptians, Bronson knows that 'Felix' still has work to do in the afterlife.

Bronson and his partners were brave men, saddened but heroic in the way they made use of their bodies in their art right up to the last possible moment and beyond. They are defiant and upbeat, certain that their art is of central political importance to the age they are living and dying in. They live with the daily spectacle of death and don't accord it too much respect. When something is as commonplace as that, you don't. It becomes a kind of tool of the trade.

For those of us who survive to contemplate this image twenty years later, however, some of the immediate political impetus that the photo itself attempted to galvanize and which formed its conditions of reception, has dissolved. The return of 'Felix' to the General Idea allows other associations to cluster around it, many of them existential. Because this image remains a 'portrait', and in any portrait it's the eyes of the sitter that give life, that focus attention. Felix's eyes are dead *and* open; and it is in this conjunction that the uncanny force of this piece of visual art resides. Indeed there is something puppet-like about his general demeanour and it was to Hoffman's doll, Olympia, that Ernst Jentsch turned in his initial attempts to theorise the uncanny, that unsettling mixture of strange and familiar.

A little later, the French philosopher of excess, Georges Bataille, would remind his readers of Robert Louis Stevenson's 'exquisite' definition of the eye as 'a cannibal delicacy', 'the object of such anxiety that we will never bite into it'. Bataille goes on to evoke the final illustrations of J. J. Grandville made shortly before his death. These depict the figures of a nightmare in which a disembodied eye observes a criminal who strikes a tree in a dark wood believing it to be a human being and from which human blood certainly flows. Again perhaps, a vision of 'Felix' as a broken and dismembered Dustie-Fute, and a tortured echo of the Rilkean tree that 'surges' in the listener's ear floats to the surface.

Above all, though, it is the embodied nature of Bronson's 'Felix' that most disturbs, a body that is dead and yet in which the traces of life remain visible. It fascinates precisely because it presents us with a view of what we most dread and most desire to see: to describe this as 'an image of our own death' is not quite right. Nor is it an image of passage or transition, despite Bronson's evocation of the 'transi'.

It is rather the way in which the photo makes death present to us as it can never be in life. Think of Dr Donne having himself painted in his shroud, although there Donne 'plays' at death while 'Felix' multitasks in a much more profound manner. We touch here on the still controversial Freudian idea of the death drive that helps to explain the repetitive actions and dreams of the trauma victim. When we catch Felix's gaze in this photograph what we see, perhaps, are the bars of a prison that has held humanity captive from the moment it understood that it was mortal and desired a literal view of that mortality.

However, this still does not account for the full power of this visual image. And it seems to me that we cannot fully appreciate it without placing it within a specific historical moment, the earlier catastrophic phase of the auto-immune deficiency syndrome.

The uncanny nature of Felix's gaze stems also from our knowledge that his deathbed was also the bed of love. I realise that this kind of remark could take us into the morally threadbare and intellectually puerile world of sociological commentary in which obscene equations were once made – and in some countries of the world continue to be made – between plague and homosexuality. My purpose in saying this, nonetheless, is simply to suggest the way in which this photograph both feeds and feeds off a century of Freudian speculation about the connection between *eros* and *thanatos*. In this respect the photograph delivers a shock of recognition: our lives and our deaths are made simultaneously present to us and held out to us, offered by Felix's gaze.

Shock and an image of prison bars were also present in my mind and that of many of my contemporaries in the early 1980s as we read the first reports of what would become known as AIDS and gradually took stock of what this meant for our love-lives and for our lives.

At that time, I spent some years living in Paris researching the life of an eighteenth-century oddball named Joseph Joubert. My days were mostly spent in the old Bibliothèque nationale in the rue de Richelieu, occasionally noticing the bald pate of Michel Foucault who often sat in an area of the library called the 'hemicyle' which was reserved for the study of rare books.

I was a much more timid figure than Foucault, and this timidity may have saved my life at the time. Gradually I became more politicised and towards the end of the eighties left the shelter of my libraries to take part in activist protests. I won't ever forget the one organised by ACT-UP, when a whole crowd of us sat down in neat rows, one behind the other, on the Boulevard de Sebastopol. We were carted off, surprisingly gently, by the CRS, the French riot police, and taken to the local nick where I was let go after a couple of hours. No one spoke harshly or insulted us but I did notice that the police never took off their gloves.

Another image that remains from those days is a visit – several visits if truth be told – to a notorious bar just off the rue de Rivoli. I must have been all of nineteen at the time but the definite chronology of these years is blurred for me now. Downstairs it was just a noisy, crowded bar. After I had managed to buy my 'demi' and been smiled at ironically by the handsome barman, I stood right at the back just watching what was going on.

Eventually I spotted what I hoped I would see: now and again men would nonchalantly stroll up some stairs at the back and disappear behind a curtain. More men went up than came down and it took me several visits to pluck up the courage to follow them.

I found myself in quite a large space divided into different rooms by partitions and curtains. It was pretty dark but my eyes adjusted eventually to all but one of the rooms, which was pitch black. I remember standing on the threshold of this room and trying to make out what was going on inside.

At first I thought it was empty but after a while I realised something was breathing or sighing. I became aware of sound first of all, and then – now and again – I made out the glimmer of an arm or a leg rising or falling. The room was filled to bursting with a mass of heaving, undulating human flesh.

Looking again at 'Felix' lying on his quilts, I can't help wondering if that glimmering darkroom could not be seen as a kind of reverse image of Bronson's photograph: moving limbs, this time, caught up in acts of ecstasy that morphed suddenly into immediate stillness.

Again, I know that saying such things takes us into the forum where homosexual 'promiscuity' is 'punished' with death. But such thoughts and statements belong to a different order of commentary. What we are dealing with here is not 'promiscuity' but an uncanny 'proximity' that characterises ontology itself. In that room, as in this photograph, life and death commingle as intimately and as naturally as light and shadow.

But that decade of discovery was also a moment of imprisonment: the realisation that we would spend a lifetime – those of us who were lucky – of living at one remove (the remove of latex) from the most immediate and intimate expression of our love for other human beings. Unless, of course, we were willing to take continual, and for very many years, immeasurable risks. Not that I was as 'marked' as those contemporaries who did not survive, of course. I have enjoyed a much longer lifetime than they.

But this is why I cannot honestly get far beyond the art of Wojnarowicz, of Mapplethorpe, of Haring or Bronson, cannot respond with poems to all those playful, postmodern, sometimes joyful sheddings of identity that characterize the final images of the *Hide and Seek* exhibition.

I do not say any of this in a pessimistic frame of mind. My accent here is not intended to be calculatingly tragic. I am simply trying to understand and articulate the nature of an existential experience. The fact is that I was caught by that era; I would say 'branded' almost, in all senses of that word.

And there is a sense in which everything since the early 1980s has been a strange kind of 'afterlife'. Is it right or sensible to make so much of that basic, sexual act? From every rational perspective, from every emotional perspective – in terms of what we owe to our families, friends and existing partners – no. But to write a new poem based on Bronson's image would involve a form of repetition of something that cannot be repeated, cannot be copied because it always accompanies you at some level of your being and because that 'original' poem is always happening, always being said.

I was going to admit to a kind of artistic impotence here but I have come to believe that there are some essential experiences – among them this experience of the prison – that you carry with you, that you constantly (although not always consciously) inhabit and that rather than attempting to 'transcend' them and 'move on' – to use the threadbare vocabulary of the agony aunt – it is better simply to remember them and, if poetry is at issue, to recite them. Recitation is not the same as repetition.

Bronson's photograph shows us something very primitive. Felix's astonished face admits to both horror and joy. He is Egyptian and he is extinction. He is the prison gate, one side of which is opening, just as the other is closing.

You thread a sea with your eye;
each time the needle enters your flank
the pain composes you;

trees that hung your voice
among these patterns
wrap your quilt in foliage;

a dog barks through the branches;
a girl's arm passes like an oar
across the sunlit patches;

now your song kneels

at the river's edge
and will not flow;

your passport head is pinned in silk.

Some Women (I)

Lilith

Just a skelf, Dad said, just a chip off the...
All I wanted to do was lie with Adam,
that big milk-toothed innocent

but whenever I got close, there was a 'tut'
like a bone snapping, then Dad would appear.
He was always walking in the garden.

One night we lost the third leg and did it.
I gave as good as I got: good to be inside
him again, his utter equal.

Dad saw – up a tree
or something. Said he'd try again.
I sit here now with owls,

claws for feet, see nothing
in the darkness. But I hear her,
(the new one, Eve) pottering about

on the other side. Adam doesn't seem to notice
that she's white and I'm black.
I can tell she's a curious bitch though

and will do for them both.
Lilith can feel it in her bones.

Cain's Wife

I was a tiller, a sower, a hoer, a sewer,
a siever, a scyther, a shearer, a reaper,
a planter, a mower, a herder, a milker,
a minder, a plougher, a thresher, a gleaner;
with no time for a name of my own.

Then he killed Abel and I was
a drifter, a tramper, a marcher, a prowler,
a runner, a walker, a hiker, a rover,
a ranger, a jogger, a beggar, a hawker;
with no time for a name of my own.

There was desert and wold,
bush and veldt, steppe and silt,
mould and dust. I was gravel.
I was pebble. I was flint. I was turf.
And I dreamed of a space

crossed by voices that raised me,
by arms that held me
and hands that offered me
to lips that kissed me
with no need for a name or a time.

Adah and Zillah

Adah works all day at her name which means 'ornament';
Zillah (or 'Shadow') mirrors the pearls and clears up
the oyster shells, ever discreet; Lamech, their husband
is up at the Temple contracting more wives.

'Two is unlucky', he says, 'three is too holy',
ignoring the two sets of twins he has fathered:
Adah has given him Jabal and Jubal.
Zillah's the mother of Naamah and Tubal.

Jabal is predictable: into silk tents
and fine cattle; Jubal has the future
lining his throat while he sings
at the trees and strums on a lyre.

Tubal is a forger, shadows his half-
brother's bronze, his charisma;
Naamah's 'the girl, the green
gowned girl' to all she bewitches.

Adah and Zillah, mothers of music
and metalwork, in the rush of their world,
sometimes catch sight of a tight little face
that reminds them of Lamech.

Not theirs, yet not his – the image
of great Papa Cain perhaps?
This is Noah, counting the pearls
in the shadows, two by two.

Sarah

Angels are good for a laugh; they come up
and they say: 'God will give you a child.'
I laugh and I say: 'I'm ninety!'

They stand up indignant, unfold their wings.
'You can't laugh at God', one says.
I laugh and I say: 'I'm ninety!'

They leave in a flap and I have a wee boy
called Isaac whose name means 'he laughs'.
I laugh and I say: 'I'm ninety!'

but his nappies need changed and he giggles a lot.
Life's been a laugh despite all the travel.
Abraham gave me to Pharaoh, then Abimelech,

passing me off as his sister. Even at ninety
I'm pretty enough to tempt rulers to slit
my old husband's pendulous wattle.

At tea-time each night we laugh at our names:
'Mother and Father of multitudes'.
I'm ninety, and he's ninety-nine.

Salt

I tasted brine on the air
the moment before I saw them. It was like
learning to swallow without shuddering
after the caravan brought
oysters to our desert.

They were out of place, out of time,
muscular yet feathery, straight-
talking and winging it. You had to take them
with a pinch of salt, though news got around.
No wonder the men of Sodom
wanted to sleep with them,
season their palate with something different.

When I peered back through the blindness,
fire and brimstone,
it was me I tasted on the desert air.
I stiffened and swallowed hard.

Rebekah

Rebekah lived for tahini, hummus, falafel and tabouleh.
'The poetry is in the pita', she often proclaimed,
her farrouge moussalab was famous.

This celebrity chef had one weakness:
she loved little Jacob more than big Essau,
the homeboy more than the hunter.

Isaac was always hungry when he came in
after the game. He shouted for Essau, 'Make me
some grub – the stuff that goes well with the beer!'

Rebekah wasted no time
and slipped her sweetest baklava
to Jacob to pass off as his own.

'Sweeten his tooth with this toffee.
Get his blessing while Essau is out.
Be your brother, slip into his skins.'

Why was Rebekah so nasty?
The Good Book is silent thereon;
but Jacob looked good in his jeans

while Essau was ginger and hairy.

Snip

Snipping off the foreskin of a crying baby's just a
snip. It cries louder but that's what babies do.
Secateurs are handy; scissors
aren't sharp enough. I tell you this

because it stopped a fight God and Moses
started in our yard one day. Moses
used his fists for everything so God decided
to punch him back. I grabbed

what came to hand and slapped the little wrinkle
against my husband's heel. They looked appalled.
Not by the blood or because a woman
had slit their precious man-child's thing

but by the little raw red bulbous head
that mewled like a mandrake in the sun.
I distinctly heard God clear his throat
before he withdrew silently behind that bush.

Deborah

Beneath palms, in the places of drawing water,
it is 100 in the shade. All day, I dole out
judgement to the villagers of Israel.

For quartering beasts on beastly land
that is not his: two pots of hummus.
For sleeping with Dan, and maybe
little Benjamin as well: a thorough
stoning. Remorse is not acceptable
in my court. Her body to be a gift
for crows. Speak ye that ride on white asses,
ye that sit in judgement and walk
by the way. My ass is white
and I give good verdicts
the elders do not have the stomach for.

I foresee a time of broken horsehoofs
by the means of prancings, and my heart
is toward Barak. Arise, Barak!
The roots of war are everywhere.
Why do you hesitate to water them?

Picture your enemies' women,
crying through the lattice:
'Why is his chariot so long in coming?
'Why tarry the wheels of his chariot?
'Yea', they return answer to themselves,

'to every man a damsel or two,
a prey of divers colours of needlework,
of divers colours of needlework on both sides,
meet for the necks of them that take the spoil.'
And then the long, long cars in the long village.

Rahab

When I asked the Jewish spies in Canaan
what I might have for sheltering them,
they replied, 'Your life.' Hardly the bargain
I had hoped, but on the game
you sometimes play for time.

What was Jericho to me in any case?
I stonewalled; these strange men didn't.
The morning after I betrayed the Canaanites
I saw huge walls of water, fish
swimming up them frantically,
jumping from the Jordan's stony bed;

I saw the Jewish army ready to cross
over. Still they paused for three whole months
to cut off foreskins and polish
the long sleek tubes of trumpets
until they gleamed. Then they came:
blowing hard six times round the city walls.

I was way ahead. I felt the rumble
of that earth-shattering shout
gather in the groins of countless men
and envied them a little. How simple:
to live in a world of falling walls.

I lay down on my bed, high
in my towered room.
I was fucked; and would survive.

The Levite's Concubine

When they raped me, they said I was second best.
All along I knew it was him
they fancied, my young husband. Our host
wouldn't have it. They could take his virgin
daughter instead but not a man who'd shared his house.

My husband, my young husband, wouldn't hear
of that. He thrust me forward and slammed the door.
I am his second wife. Now he is preparing
to cut my used-up body into twelve equal parts
to send among the tribes of Israel.

They must pay him for his sacrifice. I recall
our wedding day: how his first wife gave me to him,
a far off look in her eyes, as if she saw
our husband moving further and further away,
a man firmly out of reach, summoning his God.

Ruth

Ruth stands in the field and sees it is hot and hard and dry.
She feels she must not stop and say 'No' to Naomi.

'No,' Ruth says, and bends to gather up stray
barley heads that lie like bells,
notes lost as the harvest's hum is baled
in neighbours' barns. She works all day

careful of all that falls away,
then places her basket on the threshing floor.
At first she sees a simple glean of corn,
of grain, a glean of yellow thyme and wheat,

but as she stares a shoal of herring
weaves the wicker. Dark glass glints.
Brass shavings gleam. She sees
in part and finds her tongue.

'Where you go, I will go,' she says to Naomi.
She turns to the owner of the field,
proposes marriage, feels the kick of David
jump up the weir of generations,

the King who will love Jonathan
and the endless line of women who will give birth to God.

B & D

Bathsheba loved her bubble bath and bathed
as though it were a bain-marie, bubbling
for hours above the built-up bits of Bethlehem
in a bower she thought was private. It wasn't.

David was a dirty King whose dong danced
like a weather vane, a dick like a didgeridoo.
It nosed Bathsheba's bouquet, top note first
heart-note next, though liked the base

note best. To dab her with essential oils
was his desire, detoxify and do her
proud in oriental gourmand. David
dipped his double lollipop in a gummy

balsam, dowsed it in chypre, citrus,
fougere and green. 'Oh darling,'
breathed Bathsheba, 'my bagigi
begs an audience of your Royal Secret.

Dare you dash the downtown roofs
to share my bath with me?' David
didn't hesitate – he did her husband
in – but God buggered up their son

for doing it in sin.

The Daughters of Job

Job had wealth and three fat daughters
who shuffled their feasts from house to house.
It was her turn to bake, and her turn to batter
and her turn to butter up daughter after daughter.

They did it with quince and they did it with quiche,
quinoa and quail, quesadillas and quark.
One her said, 'Stuff all this foodstuff beginning with Q
so her 2 smirked and fished out the *xia*

(*xia* is Chinese for shrimp by the way).
Her 3 followed up with xavier steak,
and *xerem de fiesta*, topped anachronistically
with xmas cake. They were just getting to

Z when Satan strolled past, going to
and fro in the earth. 'Oh God,' he said,
'set Job a test. Blow his daughters away –
they've eaten the alphabet and they never pray.'

God huffed and puffed and emitted a wind.
Fat Job's daughters just gobbled it up.
They sucked and they sooked, made the desert
dessert, used cacti for toothpicks, blew God

a soufflé of kisses. 'You want to play rough?'
he thundered through heaven. 'I've googled
the wind and here's what you get'.
He began with a zonda, moist

tropical air to dampen their pride,
a light little zephyr to wrong-foot
fat feet. They coughed up
their tea in a *vent de midi*

and lost all their teeth in a tehuantepecer.
'Take this bhoot, this chinook, you blubbery
bags,' he said, as he sqwered them all
with a bull's eye squall.

Job didn't complain, though he sat
in his ash covered in boils.
'What's for breakfast?' he said to his wife,
'Plain porridge.'
                    'Well, thank God for that.'

King David's Concubines

No, the technical term is *hypospadias,* I think.
It sprayed and dribbled and its hooded appearance
made it look like a cobra when aroused.
It swayed around a lot. Yes. I'd call it bent.

No, definitely priapic. We had a little
box built for it that fitted underneath
his apron – I mean tunic – below his
bulge. It was always up. Yes. Tiresome.

No, he was glad to be Jewish
because of the phimosis, so
circumcision was a huge relief
all round. Insensitive? Yes. Goes with the job.

No, it was a bloodnut, a redhead,
a carrot-top with ginger minge.
He called it 'Bluey' for fun.
Yes, I just thought it was infected.

No, but it could read. It had a taste
for the Pentateuch and pronounced
the 'p' in 'psalms'. It was a prophet.
Yes, always knew what was coming.

No, it lived for others. Self-
effacing, always muffled in some
muff. Withdrew politely when asked,
yes. Said 'Bless you!' when it sneezed.

No, technologically advanced
is not the word. It let me see the world
in full HD. No analogue
could do it justice. Yes. It invented God.

No, it liked boys too. More than
ten, no doubt. There was a Jonathan
(isn't there always?) And after each
it was harder in every way. Yes,

it did away with binaries. When we touched
base-2, I couldn't count. It was strict though.
Gave me zeros and ones for everything.
Queer? Yes. Where extremes meet.

Hannah

Sometimes I smooth out my apron
against my legs. Good legs. Strong legs.
Or I stare at it as it flaps in the wind on the line.
Sometimes I stare at a tile caught by the sun

or I experiment: pull a face, play dead, pull
a face, play dead, face out the mirror
testing its stillness. I look down
then up very suddenly, trying to catch

the angel behind me, slipping out
of the frame. Why would the angel
be behind me? I ball my fist
and my nieces and nephews

– so many – hand me sprays
from the garden. Is this news?
A bird almost lands on my head.
I tuck in the stray hairs.

I close my eyes and clench myself.
Yawn with the tension of holding
everything shut. *There!* Like a nut
popping out of a shell, I am gone,

he is here, for a second, my son,
my Samuel. Sometimes
you have to be
what you want.

Some Women (II)

Martha

Och, Mary just stares up at him, like, with her big
rabbit eyes. But there's pots and pans to be cleaned
isn't there and feet to wash and corpses to lay out.
I bustle round him and he tells me you're an awful bustler,
Martha; – he remembered my name! – asks me if I think
my brother Lazarus will rise again. He'll rise again
on the day of judgement, says I. Says he, I am
the resurrection and the life. Says I, well help me
resurrect this bucket for the well. It has a hole in it
and Lazarus will need a bloody good wash
when you've finished with him.

Virgin

When I was a girl, each time I turned
a corner there was a rustling, as if
someone had just left. It was hard
to wait until I could be spoken to,
and terrifying when the child took root.

It was hard to wed an old man
just because his gift of withered branches
bloomed as I placed them on the altar.
Harder still when I noticed how the calm,
distracted boy always looked right past me
to the sunlight at the window.

The quietist activist I've ever known –
love was a miracle for him. To me
it was real, even when he noticed I was there
and turned aside. He preferred men.
Ate and laughed and slept with them.
I feared for him. I placed my hands like wings

on his head. He shrugged them off
and after supper, in a local park,
they arrested him. It was hard
to see his fine, emaciated face
when I stood beside the bier
with the disciple he loved.

Mary Magdalene

What I remember is a terrible dream
of something hanging nearby, above me,
just to the right and I couldn't look up.
There was blood. The whiteness was tremendous.

What I remember is I was weeping,
and I turned to the gardener (who looked like
my husband) and I screamed, 'The body has gone!'
He told me to look inside. 'Look within.'

Two words. So I think he meant into myself.
I tried but found nothing. Their questions
never stop. I feel my bones going off
to preach on their own, each with a slightly

different story. Some days I wear a red dress,
and sit with my alabaster jar to bring it back,
even the sins. They write it all down.
But what good will that do?

'Start again' was his favourite saying.
He didn't bleed.
The whiteness is tremendous.

First Letter of the Hebrew Women to St Paul

Hebrew Women, apostles of Christ Jesus to Paul,
alleged saint, notorious scribbler: grace to you
and peace from God our Father. Now look here:

Adam could have said 'no thanks' or 'apples
disagree with me'. He didn't. He had a bite
as well. So he was deceived. Just like Eve.

We're equal and get used to it. We washed his feet,
made his tea, stood under the cross.
Where were you? On some road to Damascus.

Useless. Chapter 2: this new covenant is all very well
but we have a soft spot for the old one. That tabernacle
had our best candlesticks in it, a gold jar

with jam by Manna and a lot of tablet. We want
it back. You promise this and you promise that.
Be quiet. Let the hidden person of the heart speak out.

Chapter the last: every Tom, Dick and Harry's
given hospitality at yours in case they might be
angels. Fine. But haven't you noticed the spinning

saucers we've got above our heads?
Faith is a stubborn doubt before what you despair of
and the conviction of things you can see with your own two eyes.

Wood

Heartwood in softwood thought of Adam
and the chair back it gave the young gardener.
Sapwood in softwood remembered the shadow
cast by the apple on bark. Springwood,
too young to recall much at all, imagined
the coming and going under the palm tree
at Timnah; and corewood still felt the essential
pain of being bush in a world thinking itself
divine. As latewood allowed a final
sparrow to take its last blood-red berry
they stiffened. Began to concentrate
on cell length, wall thickness, cellulose crystallinity.
Between them they wove their own myths
about moisture and fire. They never took earth for granted.

Orpheus. Eurydice. Hermes.

After Rilke and a photograph by PaJaMa

That was a beach at Nantucket
– The Jetties, maybe, or Eel Point Rd –
I forget. In the haar, flatness has given
up and the boardwalk ends in steps
descending. He sits down in the middle
or near the bottom, not far
from the top in fact. You could feel
the sea welling up all around; it hung
above like a soft pumice stone
and if it falls he'll wash up
in its caverns and gouges, foamy
and silver tinted. Out of the photo
there's the hint of a watery sun.

There was a hill, going
down. And a bridge-like walk-
way and the sea, the sea hanging. Have I
mentioned this before?
And behind, the long trek
of white lattice over the unstable
sand. It was like…

They must have come down this path too.

In front, he looks skinny in his blue jacket –
he looks impatient; he looks straight ahead;
he looks hungry; he looks.
The Leica camera clutched in his hands
looks back. He senses it there now,
heavy, grafting away;
though he's in two minds:

one churns like an animal turning
in its litter, never finding
its point of rest; the other
rushes forward biddably to train
the camera and snap the shutter,
its click like a muffled yap,
a shuffle of falling screens
that close then open at the echo
of their plimsolls on the sand;
those two who will follow him home.

He took the picture... still...
he's in the frame.

      ★

No. Those sounds are just ghosts
of their shapes which jut
from the dunes behind them,
his collar snuffling the wind,
the wind dashing up to his back.
He says to himself, they are
there; says it aloud; she
has crouched down; he
stands a little way off.
If only he could turn round
just once or be this camera
seeing them all
(all would be exposed
so near the end)
then they would be real,
maybe all of them,
those two, behind him,
at least:

the woman, wrapped in a nurse's
house coat, her whole body attuned
as an aerial attached to the walkway;
an abandoned instrument, she points,
and there, hand brushing the struts
that bear their weight: him

a man, whose blintering eyes blanche
everything that spreads before him
and no sound rises, no note, no
cry, an emptiness deeper
than the horizonless beach.
The mist connects them
like a winding memory
in which the other man,
far out in front, is lost.

Together, they turned
and went back to the car park,
not daring to look at one another.
She, irritable, her white coat
trailing behind her; he,
wrapped up in himself,
gesturing now and again;
the first man ignoring them both.

Perhaps they tried to remember
each other's touch,
and sunlight, turning through
the fog, caught them
like motes of dust scattered
in the rush of light
streaming from a film.

Perhaps the shower stopped it,
loosening them all, letting them

home to their own selfish thoughts.
And when, suddenly,
the woman put out her hand towards him saying,
with sorrow in her voice, *Can't you*
look back?
he did not seem to understand, and softly answered
Who?

                Anyway,
dark before the rain-spattered exit,
I or someone else stood. You could not make
me out. I stood and saw
how, on the single track over
the machair, with a sad look,
the woman turned to follow him
already walking back along the path
to the vast absent view, his footsteps
echoless, so gentle, so patient.

Text

Muhammed texts me on Scruff from Alexandria.
I mention Cavafy and he asks me when I'll visit.
I think of Egypt, Shakespeare. *Never,* I reply,
It's too far. Then I clock he means the one
in West Dunbartonshire and blush. *Cavafy
was Greek,* he says. *I'm Syrian and a refugee.*
Constantine Cavafy would have known just
what to say then from his careful room.
He dealt in exiles mainly, some refugees,
and had a knack for letting the window veil
blow back at the turn of a line
so we can see young Antony
glint briefly from his high abandoned
tower block, sense his fate blow out
along the second-best streets
of a second-hand city. Muhammed
is waiting for me to reply as I write
this poem. It is nineteen and a quarter
miles from Glasgow to Alexandria.

Scots Glossary

AIK	oak tree
AGLEY	undone
BERE	barley
CLASH	fall, crash
CREAM O THE WELL	the first water drawn from a well on New Year's Day
DEEBACK	dieback (condition affecting trees)
DWAM	dream
DUSTIE-FUTE	a merchant, a troubadour, a juggler. Here, a figure of Orpheus.
FAA	fall
FREMMIT	foreign
GOWP	throb
HAUN	hand
HAP	cover
HIDE	skin
LENTLY	slowly
LENT FEVER CRAIG	slow fever
MIRK	dark
NICHT HAWK	moth
OUTLOUP	outpour
PARAWD	procession, parade
RERR	exquisite, rare
SMEDDUM	courage
STOUR	dust
SWATCH	type, kind
THRIST	thirst
WORDY	worthy
WUN	wind

Acknowledgements

Some of these poems have appeared in *The Best British Poetry 2012* (Salt), *Blackbox Manifold*, *Flux*, *Gutter*, *Irish Pages*, *Mollosus*, *New Writing Scotland*, *Out There* (Freight, 2014), and *PN Review*. The two-part sequence 'Some Women' was first published as a pamphlet by Happenstance Press in 2014.

The Orpheus poems are a response to the exhibition *Hide and Seek: Difference and Desire in American Portraiture* that took place at the National Portrait Gallery, Washington DC in 2011. The author is grateful to its curators Jonathan Katz and David Ward for help afforded during its composition and to *The Arts and Humanities Research Council* for a Fellowship that made its writing possible.

Thanks also to Eric, Gerry McGrath, Helena Nelson, Richard Price and Robert Crawford.

Arts & Humanities
Research Council